SAVE, MAKE MORE MONEY

How to Save Money, Invest, and Live a Life of Purpose

Paul Hamdan

COPYRIGHT © [PAUL HAMDAN] [2024]

All rights reserved. No part of this book may be reproduced, stored in a retrieval system, or transmitted in any form or by any means, electronic, mechanical, photocopying, recording, or otherwise, without the prior written permission of the copyright owner.

DISCLAIMER

The information presented in this book is for general information purposes only and is not intended to be taken as professional financial advice. The author and publisher make no representations or warranties of any kind, express or implied, about the completeness, accuracy, reliability, suitability, or availability of the information contained in this book.

In no event will the author or publisher be liable for any loss or damage, including but not limited to indirect or consequential loss or damage, or any loss or damage whatsoever arising from loss of data or profits arising out of or in connection with the use of this book.

The information in this book is subject to change without notice. The author and publisher are not responsible for any errors or omissions in this book.

ABOUT THE AUTHOR

Paul Hamdan is a financial expert, author, and passionate advocate for financial literacy. With years of experience in the financial industry, Paul has helped countless individuals and families achieve their financial goals and build a brighter financial future.

Paul's mission is to empower people with the knowledge and skills they need to take control of their finances and make smart financial decisions. He believes that financial freedom is within everyone's reach, and he is dedicated to helping people achieve it.

In his book "Save, Make More Money", Paul shares his expertise and provides a comprehensive guide to saving money, investing, and building wealth. With his clear and concise writing style, Paul makes complex financial concepts accessible to everyone, regardless of their financial background or expertise.

Paul's work has been featured in various media outlets and financial publications, and he is a sought-after speaker on financial topics. He lives with his family and is committed to continuing to educate and inspire people to take control of their finances and achieve financial freedom.

ACKNOWLEDGEMENTS

I would like to express my heartfelt gratitude to my family, whose unwavering support and encouragement have been a constant source of inspiration throughout my writing journey. Without their love and understanding, this book would not have been possible.

I am also deeply grateful to my friends, who have provided valuable feedback, guidance, and motivation at every stage of the writing process. Their contributions have been invaluable, and I am fortunate to have them in my life.

Additionally, I would like to acknowledge the work of several authors whose writings have had a profound impact on my own understanding of personal finance and wealth creation. The insights and principles shared by experts like Dave Ramsey, Robert Kiyosaki, and Tony Robbins have been instrumental in shaping my ideas and approaches, and I am grateful for their contributions to the field.

Thank you all again for your support and contributions. I am grateful and humbled by the opportunity to share my ideas and expertise with you, the reader.

Sincerely,
Paul Hamdan

CONTENTS

INTRODUCTION 11
PART 1: FOUNDATIONS OF FINANCIAL FREEDOM... 13
    1.1 Why Saving Money Matters 14
    1.2 Assessing Your Finances and Setting Goals.... 16
    1.3 Creating a Budget That Works for You 21
PART 2: SAVING MONEY STRATEGIES 25
    2.1: Cutting Back on Unnecessary Expenses 26
    2.2: Saving Money on Everyday Items 29
    2.3: Reducing Debt and Building an Emergency Fund 32
PART 3: INVESTING FOR THE FUTURE 35
    3.1: Introduction to Investing and Risk Management.. 36
    3.2: Building a Diversified Investment Portfolio 39
    3.3: Growing Your Wealth Through Compound Interest 44
PART 4: SMART MONEY MOVES 48
    4.1: How to Save Money on Big Purchases 49
    4.2: Smart Ways to Shop for Everyday Items 53
    4.3: Avoiding Financial Pitfalls and Scams 57
PART 5: BUILDING MULTIPLE INCOME STREAM... 62
5.1: Starting a Side Hustle or Freelancing 63
    5.2: Investing in Real Estate or Dividend-Paying Stocks 66
    5.3: Creating Passive Income Streams 70

PART 6: LIVING A LIFE OF PURPOSE...................... 74
    6.1: Aligning Your Finances with Your Values..........74

    6.2: Pursuing Your Passions and Living a Fulfilling Life.. 78

    6.3: Giving Back and Making a Positive Impact......82

PART7: OVERCOMING OBSTACLES AND STAYING MOTIVATED.. 86

7.1: Overcoming Financial Setbacks and Staying Disciplined...87

    7.2: Staying Motivated and Focused on Your Goals... 90

    7.3: Building a Supportive Community and Network.. 93

PART 8: PUTTING IT ALL TOGETHER.................... 100
    8.1: Creating a Long-Term Financial Plan............ 101

    8.2: Reviewing and Adjusting Your Progress........105

    8.3: Achieving Financial Freedom and Living a Life of Purpose.. 107

Conclusion... 112

INTRODUCTION

Consider yourself at a crossroads, with two paths extending out before you. One path is trodden and familiar, leading to a life of financial hardship and insecurity. The alternative path is less frequented, yet it holds promise for a life of financial freedom and stability. As you stand there, you can feel the weight of your financial obligations pressing down on you. Your debt is increasing, your funds are decreasing, and your financial future is uncertain. You realize you need to make a change, but you're not sure where to start.

That is where this book comes in. "Save, Make More Money" is your path to financial independence. It's a step-by-step guide that will teach you how to:

- Manage your funds effectively
- Eliminate debt and create a safety net
- Invest in passive income-generating assets
- Create several revenue sources for financial stability
- Live a life that is consistent with your values and ambitions.

With the tactics and practices in this book, you'll be able to break free from the bonds of financial stress and attain the financial independence you deserve. You'll be able to live the life you want without fear of financial constraints. So, let's begin your journey to financial freedom today!

PART 1: FOUNDATIONS OF FINANCIAL FREEDOM

1.1 Why Saving Money Matters

Saving money is an essential part of obtaining financial stability, security, and freedom. Individuals who do not grasp its value risk sliding into the trap of living paycheck to paycheck, plagued by debt, and worried about their financial future. Saving money is more than just putting aside a portion of your salary; it's about creating a safety net, a cushion to shield you from life's unforeseen twists and turns. It is about having the financial freedom to follow your goals, dreams, and aspirations without being hampered by financial limitations.

Saving money is more than just deferring satisfaction; it's an investment in yourself, your family, and your future. You're laying the groundwork for long-term financial progress, which will act as a catapult to reaching your financial goals. Saving money also brings peace of mind. It is the awareness that you have a financial cushion, or reserve, that will allow you to face life's obstacles with confidence and composure. It is the assurance that you can weather financial storms, that you are prepared for the unforeseen, and that you have a strategy in place to reach your financial objectives.

Furthermore, saving money helps you to have control over your financial future. It's a declaration of debt freedom, a pledge to create a better financial future. It's a mentality shift, recognizing that you're the mastermind behind your financial success and have the ability to shape your financial destiny. Saving money is essential for reaching financial freedom. It's the key to realizing your financial potential, pursuing your aspirations, and living a life that reflects who you are. Prioritizing savings is an investment in yourself, your family, and your future. You are creating a financial legacy that will reflect your financial acumen and caution.

Remember that saving money is more than a financial habit; it is an attitude, a philosophy, and a way of life. It is a dedication to living below your means, prioritizing your financial goals, and laying a solid financial foundation for the future. So, make saving money a priority and watch your financial future change in ways you never imagined.

1.2 Assessing Your Finances and Setting Goals

Taking control of your finances is an important step toward financial freedom. It is a process that demands honesty, dedication, and a thorough awareness of your financial status.

Assessing your money and making goals is the first step toward a better financial future. The first step in analyzing your finances is to collect all pertinent financial data. This contains your income, expenses, debts, credit reports, and other financial records. It is critical to have a comprehensive view of your financial status, including areas where you may be overspending or struggling to make ends meet.

Once you've gathered all of the essential information, it's time to develop a budget. A budget is a tool that allows you to successfully manage your finances and ensure that your resources are allocated appropriately. It is not a spending limit, but rather a guideline to help you make informed financial decisions. When making a budget, it's critical to separate your expenses into needs and wants. Rent, utilities, and groceries are examples of necessities, whereas desires are discretionary expenses such as entertainment and hobbies. Prioritizing your needs over your wants allows you to better utilize your resources.

After generating a budget, it's time to set financial objectives. Goals provide direction and concentration, allowing you to stay motivated and committed to your financial objectives. When setting goals, ensure that they are explicit, quantifiable, achievable, relevant, and time-bound. Short-term goals should include paying off debt, saving for emergencies, and boosting your credit score. Long-term goals should include wealth growth, retirement preparation, and financial independence. Once you've determined your goals, it's time to devise a strategy to reach them. This strategy should contain measures for debt reduction, investing, and asset accumulation. It's critical to be realistic and adaptable, because your plan may need to be modified when your financial situation changes.

Assessing your finances and setting goals is an important step toward financial freedom. By taking control of your finances, developing a budget, and setting SMART objectives, you'll be able to successfully manage your resources, attain financial stability, and build a better financial future.

Here are some key takeaways to keep in mind:

To take control of your finances, gather all relevant financial information.
- create a budget that prioritizes necessities over wants.
 -Set SMART financial objectives that are clear, measurable, realistic, relevant, and time-bound.
- Create a plan to attain your goals, such as debt reduction, investing, and wealth creation.
- Be realistic and flexible, as your financial circumstances may require adjustments.
Remember that reviewing your money and setting goals is a continuous process. It takes constant monitoring and modifications to ensure you're on pace to meet your financial goals. By remaining motivated and focused, you can attain financial independence and a brighter financial future.

1.3 Creating a Budget That Works for You

A budget is an efficient tool for managing your finances, achieving financial stability, and meeting financial goals. In this chapter, we'll look at how to construct a budget that works for you rather than against you.

Understanding Your Spending Habits

Before constructing a budget, you must first analyze your spending habits. For one month, record every single transaction you make, even modest expenditures like coffee or snacks. This will assist you in identifying areas where you may minimize costs and utilize resources more effectively.

Categorizing Your Expenses

Organize your spending into categories, like:
   - Housing (rent or mortgage, utilities, maintenance)
   - Transportation (vehicle loan, gas, and insurance; public transportation)
- Food (grocery, dining out)
- Insurance (health, life, and disability).
- Debt (credit cards or loans)

- Entertainment (hobbies, films, concerts)
- Savings (emergency fund and retirement)

Assigning Percentages

Determine a percentage of your money for each category based on your priorities and financial objectives. A general guideline is:
- Housing: 30%.
- Transportation (10%)
- Food: 10%
- Insurance: 5 percent.
- Debt: 5%
- Entertainment (5%).
- Save 10%

Creating a Budget Plan

Use the 50/30/20 rule to allocate:
- Spend 50% of your income on basic expenses (housing, utilities, food).
 - 30% for discretionary spending (entertainment and hobbies).
 - 20% for savings and debt repayment.

Tracking Your Expenses

Use a budgeting app, spreadsheet, or simply a notebook to track your expenses. Regularly review your spending to ensure you're staying within your allocated percentages.

Adjusting and Refining

Adjust your budget to reflect your changing financial circumstances. Life is unpredictable, thus your budget should be adaptable enough to adjustments.
By following these steps, you'll be able to design a budget that works for you, allowing you to achieve financial stability, minimize stress, and achieve your financial objectives.
A person sits at a desk, surrounded by budgeting instruments (calculator, notebook, budgeting app on their phone), with a contented look, showing they have made a budget that works for them.

PART 2: SAVING MONEY STRATEGIES

2.1: Cutting Back on Unnecessary Expenses

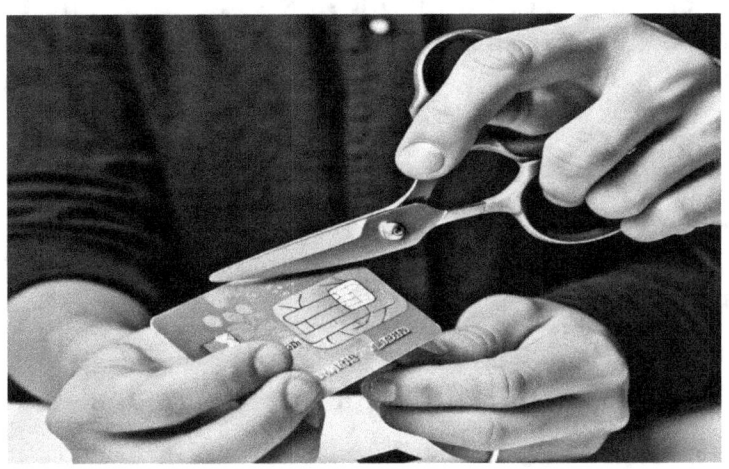

Creating a budget is an important step toward financial security, but it's just half of the battle. The next phase is to reduce superfluous expenses and deploy resources more efficiently. This needs discipline, self-awareness, and a determination to change. Begin by reviewing your spending habits and identifying places where you may cut back. Ask yourself, "Do I really need this?" or "Can I find a cheaper alternative?". Be true to yourself, and don't be afraid to make compromises.

Discretionary spending, such as dining out, entertainment, and hobbies, is sometimes one of the most significant areas for savings. These charges can easily accumulate and deplete your budget.

Consider alternatives such as cooking at home, finding free or low-cost entertainment, and trying new activities that aren't too expensive. Another thing to consider is your daily habits. Do you visit a coffee shop every morning for a latte? Do you purchase a newspaper or magazine every day? These tiny expenses may appear inconsequential, but they can accumulate over time. Consider brewing your own coffee at home or switching to a digital subscription for news and entertainment.

Cutting back on unnecessary costs necessitates a mentality adjustment. Instead of thinking "I deserve this" or "I've earned it," consider "Do I really need this?" or "Can I find a better use for my money?". Remember that every dollar you save can be used to achieve your financial goals.

Cutting back on unnecessary spending allows you to better use your resources, make progress toward your financial goals, and achieve financial stability.

Consider the following tips to help you save unnecessary expenses:

- Use the envelope approach to categorize your expenses and stay inside your budget. - Instead of using credit, save up and pay in cash for large purchases.

- Use a price comparison tool to guarantee you're getting the greatest value on daily necessities.

- Consider purchasing used or refurbished things rather than new ones.

- Use budgeting software to keep track of your expenses and avoid overspending.

- Implement a "one in, one out" strategy for your stuff to reduce clutter and unneeded purchases.

- Increase your savings by participating in a savings challenge, such as the "52-week savings challenge".

- Consider downsizing or decluttering your living area to cut costs such as rent and electricity.
- Consult a financial planner or advisor to help you make sound financial decisions.

Implementing these tactics will allow you to reduce wasteful spending, better organize your resources, and attain financial stability.

2.2: Saving Money on Everyday Items

Saving money on everyday things is an excellent method to reduce costs and better allocate your resources. Making a few simple changes to your daily habits and shopping routine can help you save money on the goods you need and want.

Here are some methods for saving money on everyday items:

- Buy in bulk: Buying groceries, household supplies, and personal care products in bulk can save you money over time.

- Use discounts and discount codes: discounts, discount codes, and cashback applications can help you save money on everyday purchases.
- Shop during sales: Plan your shopping visits around sales to stock up on non-perishable items and save money.
- Enroll in retailer loyalty programs to earn points, perks, and discounts on your routine purchases.
- Purchase generic or store-brand products: Generic or store-brand products are typically less expensive than name-brand products while providing comparable quality. - Avoid impulse purchases: Stick to your grocery list to save money and reduce waste.
- Use cashback applications: You can get money back on regular purchases by using apps like Ibotta, Fetch Rewards, and Rakuten.
- Buy in season: Buying produce in season will help you save money on fresh fruits and vegetables.

- Use unit prices: Compare prices by unit (price per ounce or pound) to verify you're receiving the best value.
- Avoid shopping while hungry: Buying groceries on a full stomach allows you to avoid impulsive purchases and stick to your shopping list.

2.3: Reducing Debt and Building an Emergency Fund

Reducing debt and creating an emergency fund are critical steps toward financial stability and security. Paying off high-interest debt and establishing a safety net can better prepare you to deal with unforeseen expenses and achieve your long-term financial goals.

Here are some ideas to help you minimize debt and create an emergency fund:

Reducing debt:

- Develop a debt repayment strategy: Prioritize your loans based on interest rate, focusing on paying off high-interest debt first.
- Pay more than the minimum: Make additional payments to reduce principal balances and interest costs over time.
- Consider debt consolidation: Combine several debts into a single loan with a lower interest rate and a single monthly payment. - Reduce costs and direct more income toward debt repayment.

Building an Emergency Fund:
- Set a goal: Save 3-6 months of living expenses in an easily accessible savings account.
- Start small: Set a modest goal, such as saving $1,000, then progressively expand your ambition.
- Automate Savings: Schedule regular transfers from your checking account to your emergency fund.
- Avoid tapping into savings: Keep your emergency fund separate and only use it for true situations.

Remember that lowering debt and creating an emergency fund require time and discipline, but the financial peace of mind they provide is well worth the effort.

PART 3: INVESTING FOR THE FUTURE

3.1: Introduction to Investing and Risk Management

Investing is a vital element of reaching long-term financial goals including retirement, home ownership, and education finance. However, investing has hazards, and understanding how to manage those risks is critical to ensuring that your investments are in line with your financial goals.

Understanding Investing

Investing is the act of placing money into assets with a high chance of increasing in value over time. The idea is to achieve returns that surpass inflation, increasing your spending power. Investing can be difficult, especially for beginners, but starting early allows you to take advantage of compound interest.

Types of Investments

There are different forms of investments, each with its own qualities, rewards, and hazards. Stocks represent ownership in firms and have the potential for long-term growth. Bonds are debt obligations that provide regular revenue while posing relatively low risk. Real estate investing generates rental income or property appreciation, whereas mutual funds and exchange-traded funds (ETFs) offer diverse portfolios. Commodities and currencies provide various investment opportunities.

Risk Management

Risk management is an important component of investing since it protects your money and allows you to reach your financial objectives. Risk management entails recognizing, evaluating, and managing potential hazards. Market risk, credit risk, liquidity risk, inflation risk, and interest rate risk are all frequent hazards for investors. Diversification, asset allocation, hedging, regular portfolio rebalancing, and a long-term perspective are all successful risk management strategies. Diversification involves spreading assets across asset classes, sectors, and locations to reduce exposure to any single risk. Asset allocation allocates investments based on risk tolerance, time horizon, and goals. Hedging employs derivatives or other assets to mitigate future losses. Regular portfolio rebalancing ensures that your portfolio remains in line with your planned asset allocation. A long-term approach focuses on long-term growth while limiting the consequences of short-term market fluctuation.

Developing a thorough understanding of investing and risk management is critical for financial success. You'll be more equipped to make informed decisions and traverse the investing landscape if you understand the fundamentals of investing, are familiar with various investment possibilities, and adopt good risk management measures. When making investment decisions, always think about your financial goals, risk tolerance, and time horizon first.

3.2: Building a Diversified Investment Portfolio

A diverse investment portfolio is an essential component of long-term financial success. You may reduce risk while increasing returns by diversifying your assets across asset classes, sectors, and locations. A well-crafted portfolio helps you handle market changes, limits exposure to any single investment, and corresponds with your financial objectives. A diversified portfolio should include a variety of asset classes, including stocks, bonds, real estate, and alternatives. Stocks have the potential for long-term gain, whilst bonds provide consistent income and a reduced risk. Real estate investing generates rental income or property appreciation, whereas commodities and currencies give protection against inflation and market volatility. Within each asset class, it is critical to diversify further by selecting a variety of investments to decrease exposure to any single stock, bond, or industry. For example, a stock portfolio should comprise a mix of large-cap, mid-cap, and small-cap equities from various sectors and businesses. This helps to reduce reliance on any one company or sector, hence reducing potential losses. Geographic diversification is also key, with investments made in both domestic and international markets to capitalize on global growth prospects. This reduces exposure to any certain economy or region, resulting in a more stable portfolio.

Regular portfolio rebalancing is essential for maintaining your intended asset allocation. As markets vary, your portfolio may become unbalanced, and rebalancing helps to restore the original allocation. This method ensures that your investments remain in line with your financial objectives, risk tolerance, and time horizon. Creating a diverse portfolio necessitates a deliberate and strategic strategy. The process begins with an assessment of your financial condition, which includes your income, expenses, assets, and liabilities. This helps to estimate your investing capacity and risk tolerance.

Next, establish specific financial goals that define your objectives, risk tolerance, and time horizon. This will assist guide your investing decisions and ensure that your portfolio meets your needs. Determine your asset allocation by splitting your investments into asset groups based on your objectives and risk tolerance. This will allow you to establish a balance between growth and stability. Choose a mix of investments from each asset class, diversifying across sectors, industries, and regions. This will help decrease exposure to any single investment, resulting in a more stable portfolio.

Regularly assess your portfolio and rebalance as needed to stay within your intended asset allocation. This ensures that your investments remain consistent with your financial objectives and risk tolerance. When constructing your portfolio, take into account other important variables besides diversification. Investment expenses, tax ramifications, and risk-management methods should all be considered. Investment expenses, such as management fees and trading commissions, might reduce your profits. To cut costs, consider low-cost index funds or exchange-traded funds (ETFs). Tax considerations can have an influence on your portfolio. Consider the tax efficiency of your investments and strive to reduce tax payments.

Risk management measures, such as hedging and diversification, can help to mitigate possible losses. Consider investing in assets that respond differently in different market scenarios to create a more stable portfolio. Building a diverse investment portfolio will help you understand the complexity of investing and achieve your long-term financial objectives. Remember to examine and rebalance your portfolio on a regular basis to verify that it is still in line with your objectives. With a well-designed portfolio, you can weather market swings and achieve financial success.

3.3: Growing Your Wealth Through Compound Interest

Being consistent is also important. Regularly adding to your investments allows you to take advantage of compound interest, which allows your wealth to grow at an increasing rate over time. It is critical to make saving and investing a habit rather than a one-off event. Choosing high-yield investments is also crucial. Choosing assets with competitive interest rates or returns increases the power of compound interest. This includes high-yield savings accounts, certificates of deposit, and stock market investments. Leaving your investments alone is also important. Allowing your investments to grow untouched, with no withdrawals or sales, helps to optimize the benefits of compound interest. This might be tough, particularly during periods of market volatility, but it is critical to maintain a long-term view.

Tax-advantaged accounts, such as a 401(k), IRA, or Roth IRA, can also help you build wealth through compound interest. These accounts provide tax benefits, which can help your assets grow more quickly over time. Monitoring and altering your assets is also necessary. Periodically monitoring your investments and rearranging as appropriate ensures that your wealth grows over time through compound interest. Educating oneself about investment and personal money is also essential. Continuously learning about new investing options and methods allows you to leverage the potential of compound interest.

Avoiding costs is also important. Minimizing investment costs helps to maximize returns, allowing your money to expand more quickly over time. Diversifying your portfolio is also necessary. Spreading investments across asset classes reduces risk and increases the power of compound interest. Finally, having patience is essential. Compound interest is a long-term approach, and you must be willing to wait for your wealth to develop. Compound interest can help you reach your financial goals over time and with consistency.

SAVE,MAKE MORE MONEY

PART 4: SMART MONEY MOVES

4.1: How to Save Money on Big Purchases

Saving money on large purchases necessitates a combination of study, planning, and effective buying methods. One major strategy is to distinguish between needs and wants, prioritizing critical products above discretionary ones. This helps to avoid impulse purchases and ensures that each large purchase is in line with budgetary goals. Researching items and comparing costs is another important step in saving money on large purchases. This can be accomplished by reading reviews, searching online marketplaces, and visiting physical stores to obtain an idea of the going prices for a specific item. Comparing costs helps you find the greatest discounts and avoid overpaying for an item.

Considering alternatives such as reconditioned or used items might also result in big savings. Refurbished items, for example, have been inspected and certified by the manufacturer or a third-party refurbisher, and they frequently come with warranties. Used things, on the other hand, may necessitate further research and examination to ensure they are in good shape, but they can result in significant savings. Purchasing wisely, such as during sales or holiday specials, can also result in significant savings. Many retailers provide special bargains and discounts at specific times of the year, such as Black Friday or Cyber Monday. Furthermore, using cashback apps, reward programs, and other incentives can result in additional savings.

Considering alternatives such as reconditioned or used items may also result in significant savings. Refurbished items, for example, have been inspected and certified by the manufacturer or a third-party refurbisher, and they usually come with a warranty. Used items, on the other hand, may require further investigation and examination to verify they are in good condition, but they can result in substantial savings. Purchasing smartly, such as during sales or holiday promotions, can also result in big savings. Many retailers offer special deals and discounts during certain times of the year, such as Black Friday and Cyber Monday. Furthermore, cashback apps, loyalty programs, and other incentives might lead to additional savings.

Finally, avoiding impulse purchases and taking the time to think critically about each purchase reduces unnecessary spending and ensures that large purchases are in line with financial goals. This involves discipline and patience, but can result in large long-term savings. In addition to these tactics, there are a number of other ways to save money on large purchases. For example, taking into account energy efficiency and durability can help you save money in the long run. Energy-efficient appliances, for example, may be more expensive initially, but they can save money on power costs over time. Similarly, while sturdy things may be more expensive at first, they can last longer and require fewer replacements.

Another option is to consider purchasing the previous year's model or a little older version of an item. Many retailers hold clearance deals on outdated models to make place for new inventory, which can result in substantial savings. Furthermore, acquiring an open-box or showcase item can result in discounts, provided the item is still in acceptable shape. Finally, using a price tracker or price comparison tool might help you find the greatest bargains and avoid paying too much for an item. These programs can notify you when the price of an item reduces or recommend similar things at a reduced cost.

4.2: Smart Ways to Shop for Everyday Items

Shopping for common products might be a tedious process, but with a few clever tactics, you can transform it into an art form! Imagine walking out of the store feeling like a clever shopper, knowing you got the greatest value on the items you needed. It's all about being aware of your purchasing patterns and making a few simple modifications to your buying routine.

First, let's discuss the value of planning. Take a few minutes before going to the store to consider what you actually need. Create a list and stick to it! This will allow you to avoid impulse purchases and keep focused on your purchasing goals. Of course, always check for sales and coupons before you leave. A little prep work can go a long way in saving you money.

Now, let us discuss the store itself. Have you ever noticed how some products are displayed at eye level while others are tucked away on higher or lower shelves? That is no accident! Stores frequently display the most expensive things at eye level, anticipating that you will grab them without thinking twice. Do not fall for it! Take a deeper look at the shelves above and below, and you might discover a better deal.

Then there's the age-old question: should you buy in quantity. The answer is: It depends! If you use a lot of anything that isn't perishable, buying in bulk can help you save money. However, if you are unsure if you will use it all before it expires, choose a smaller quantity.

Think about it: do you really need 12 cereal boxes or 6 jars of pasta sauce? Probably not.

Another item to consider is the store layout. Have you ever observed how certain goods are arranged in a precise order? That is not a coincidence! Stores frequently place the most profitable things at the end of the aisle, expecting you'll pick them up on your way out. Do not fall for it! Take a closer look at the products on the shelf and compare pricing. You might be shocked by what you discover.

Then there's the issue with brand names. Is it really necessary to buy the name-brand version of something, or will a generic version suffice? In most circumstances, the generic equivalent is equally as excellent, if not superior! Why pay extra for a fancy label? Make an informed decision and choose the generic version. Finally, let's discuss purchasing online. With only a few clicks, you can now find fantastic bargains faster than ever before. However, be aware that certain online shops may charge more for shipping than you would in-store. Always consider this when making purchasing selections. Don't forget to look for coupons and promo codes before you checkout!

By following these basic tactics, you can transform daily shopping into a smart and intelligent experience. Happy shopping! In addition to these suggestions, there are a few other things to keep in mind when shopping for everyday necessities. Consider buying during the season. Seasonal produce is frequently less expensive than out-of-season stuff, and it is also fresher! Also, remember to use cashback apps and rewards programs to get money back on your purchases.

Another thing to consider is the store's return policies. If you are unsure whether you will enjoy something, ensure that you can return it if necessary. Always check the expiration dates of perishable foods to ensure you're receiving the greatest deal. Finally, shop at local retailers or farmers' markets. You're not only helping your local community, but you're also more likely to find fresher, higher-quality products. Who knows, you might find a new favorite item.

By following these guidelines and being attentive of your buying patterns, you can make everyday shopping a smart and sensible endeavor. Happy shopping!

4.3: Avoiding Financial Pitfalls and Scams

To avoid financial hazards and scams, you must be financially literate, skeptical, and proactive. In today's complex financial landscape, you must be aware of potential threats to your financial well-being. Financial risks, ranging from fraudulent schemes to costly mistakes, can be disastrous. However, by knowing the risks and taking preventative measures, you can escape financial calamity and attain long-term financial security.

Fraudulent schemes are a major financial risk. Scammers frequently employ sophisticated strategies to dupe unsuspecting victims, and the repercussions can be serious. To prevent falling victim to these frauds, it is critical to exercise caution when dealing with unsolicited offers or investment opportunities. Always conduct comprehensive research on the company or individual, and never give out personal financial information to someone you do not trust.

Another financial risk is high-interest debt, which can lead to a difficult-to-break debt cycle. Credit cards, payday loans, and other high-interest financing choices may be appealing, but they may easily become out of hand. To escape this trap, utilize credit wisely and pay on time. If you're dealing with debt, think about combining your loans or seeing a credit counselor. In addition to fraudulent schemes and high-interest debt, there are numerous other financial traps to avoid. Investment fraud, identity theft, financial planning blunders, and insurance frauds are all possible threats to your financial stability.

To prevent these financial hazards, you must be proactive and take precautions to protect yourself. Educating yourself on personal money, investment, and financial planning is essential. Diversifying your investments, setting aside an emergency fund, and routinely reviewing your credit reports can all help you stay safe. Being wary of unsolicited offers and getting professional guidance when necessary can help you escape financial ruin. Understanding the risks and taking steps to protect yourself can help you avoid financial traps and frauds and achieve long-term financial stability. Remember to exercise caution, educate yourself, and seek professional counsel when necessary. With the correct knowledge and techniques, you may create a secure financial future and achieve your financial objectives.

SAVE,MAKE MORE MONEY

PART 5: BUILDING MULTIPLE INCOME STREAM

5.1: Starting a Side Hustle or Freelancing

Starting a side hustle or freelancing may be an exciting endeavor, with the potential of extra income, creative expression, and a sense of accomplishment. But where do you begin? How can you transform your passion into a commercial endeavor? The journey may appear difficult, but with the appropriate mindset and methods, you can transform your side hustle into a profitable and lasting business.

First and foremost, discover your strengths and passions. What are you good at? What do you love doing in your spare time? These questions can help you restrict your possibilities and find a profitable niche. Perhaps you're a writer with a talent for creating compelling material, or a designer with an eye for visual storytelling. Whatever your talent, there is probably a market for it.

Once you've defined your area of expertise, you can begin developing your personal brand. This entails establishing a professional online presence, which includes a website or blog, social media profiles, and a portfolio of your work. Your brand should embody your principles, personality, and distinct selling point (USP). What differentiates you from others in your field? What differentiates your services?

Next, you'll need to create a business plan that outlines your objectives, target market, pricing, and marketing strategies. This will serve as your road map, directing your decisions and keeping you focused on your goals. Make sure to analyze your competitors, understand your target audience's needs, and tailor your strategy accordingly. Now it's time to start marketing your services and recruiting customers. This can be accomplished through a variety of methods, including social media, content marketing, email marketing, and networking events. Your goal is to establish a strong internet presence, position oneself as an expert in your sector, and generate leads. Prepare to put in the effort, as marketing is a continuous process that necessitates continual effort.

When you first start landing clients and assignments, it's critical to offer high-quality work that exceeds expectations. This will help you establish a solid reputation, get referrals, and gain repeat business. Remember that your goal is to build a sustainable business, not a fast cure. You will face challenges and setbacks along the road. Don't get discouraged; they're a necessary part of the journey. Instead, learn from your mistakes, adjust to changes, and continue on. remain current with industry trends, best practices, and new tools to remain ahead of the competition.

Starting a side hustle or freelancing needs a willingness to take risks, be adaptable, and embrace ambiguity. It's a path that requires hard effort, devotion, and perseverance. However, those that persevere can reap enormous benefits, including financial freedom, creative fulfillment, and a feeling of purpose. So, start establishing your side hustle today!

5.2: Investing in Real Estate or Dividend-Paying Stocks

Investing in real estate or dividend-paying companies is an excellent strategy to accumulate wealth and earn passive income. Both solutions have distinct advantages and disadvantages, and it is critical to understand them before making a selection. Real estate investing can provide a consistent source of income through rental properties, as well as possible long-term gain in property value. However, it demands a considerable initial investment, as well as continuing expenses such as maintenance, property taxes, and insurance. Furthermore, the real estate market can be unpredictable, with market changes influencing property values.

Dividend-paying stocks, on the other hand, provide a consistent source of income in the form of dividend payments, as well as the possibility for long-term capital appreciation. Dividend equities are less volatile than growth stocks and can provide a relatively consistent source of income. However, the dividend yield may not keep up with inflation, and there is always the possibility that the company would reduce or abolish dividend payments.

When considering investing in real estate or dividend-paying companies, you should examine your financial objectives, risk tolerance, and investment horizon. If you want a consistent source of income and are willing to take on additional risk, real estate investing could be a suitable fit. Dividend-paying stocks, on the other hand, may be a better option for those looking for a more liquid investment with a somewhat steady source of income. Finally, a well-diversified investment portfolio that includes both real estate and dividend-paying equities will help you reach your financial objectives while minimizing risk. It is critical to contact a financial counselor or investment specialist to identify the optimal investment strategy for your specific situation.

Dividend-paying stocks are popular among income-focused investors because they provide a consistent stream of income as well as the possibility for long-term capital appreciation. Real estate investing, on the other hand, provides a consistent stream of income from rental properties as well as the possibility for long-term property value appreciation. Both solutions have distinct advantages and disadvantages, and it is critical to understand them before making a selection. Real estate investing necessitates a large initial investment as well as continuous expenses like maintenance, property taxes, and insurance. However, it can provide a consistent source of income as well as the possibility for long-term property value appreciation. The real estate market can be volatile, and market swings can impact property values.

Dividend-paying equities are less volatile than growth stocks and can provide a relatively consistent source of income. However, the dividend yield may not keep up with inflation, and there is always the possibility that the company would reduce or abolish dividend payments. When considering investing in real estate or dividend-paying equities, it is critical to first determine your financial goals, risk tolerance, and investment horizon. A well-diversified investment portfolio that includes both real estate and dividend-paying companies will help you meet your financial objectives while minimizing risk. Consulting with a financial advisor or investment specialist can help you establish the best investing strategy for your specific situation.

5.3: Creating Passive Income Streams

Creating passive income streams is a dream for many people, and with good reason. Who wouldn't want to make money while sleeping, traveling, or simply enjoying life? Passive income streams can offer financial independence, security, and peace of mind. But how do you make them? First, let us define passive income. Passive income refers to earnings that require little or no work to keep. It is money that comes in on a regular basis without requiring you to actively work for it. Doesn't that sound amazing?

Now, let's go over how to build these streams. The goal is to invest your time and money carefully, so you can reap the rewards later. This may need some initial effort, but believe us when we say it is well worth it. Real estate investing is a common strategy to generate passive income. Owning rental properties allows you to earn money without actually working for it. Of course, there are certain obligations associated with being a landlord, but the rewards can be substantial.

Dividend-paying equities provide another source of passive income. You can generate a constant stream of income by investing in well-established firms with a track record of paying dividends. This is an excellent choice for individuals new to investing because it is generally low-risk and simple to grasp.

Peer-to-peer lending is another way to generate passive income. Lending money to individuals or businesses through platforms like Lending Club or Prosper allows you to earn interest on your investment. This method involves some due research but can be a consistent source of income.

Creating and selling digital assets like ebooks, courses, or software can also result in passive revenue. Once you've built the product, you may sell it and make money without having to labor for it. This method needs some imagination and knowledge, but it may be quite rewarding. Finally, affiliate marketing is a means to get passive revenue. You can earn a sales commission by recommending other firms' products or services. This method needs some marketing skills, but it can be a terrific way to make money without having to build your own items.

PART 6: LIVING A LIFE OF PURPOSE

6.1: Aligning Your Finances with Your Values

Aligning your finances with your principles is an essential step toward financial freedom and a satisfying life. Your values are the principles that influence your decisions and behaviors, and they should be reflected in the way you handle your finances. When your finances are in line with your ideals, you will feel more meaningful, confident, and satisfied. Understanding your beliefs is the first step toward ensuring that your money reflects them. Take some time to reflect on what is most important to you in life. Do you prioritize freedom, security, creativity, or community? Are you passionate about environmental sustainability, social justice, or personal development? Your values could be linked to your relationships, health, work, or personal development.

Once you have a firm understanding of your values, you can start assessing your financial circumstances and making changes to fit with them. This may entail reevaluating your spending patterns, investments, and financial objectives. Consider whether your current financial habits are in line with or contrary to your values. For example, if you value environmental sustainability, you might want to explore investing in renewable energy or lowering your carbon footprint by limiting your air travel. If you value community, you might choose to prioritize spending on activities that bring you closer to your loved ones, such as family trips or community events.

Aligning your finances with your ideals necessitates a responsible attitude to consumption. Be honest with yourself about what you truly need versus what you desire. Consider whether each purchase is consistent with your values and helps you achieve your long-term objectives. Avoid impulse purchases and instead invest in items that will provide you long-term satisfaction and fulfillment. Your values should also guide your investment choices. Consider investing in firms that share your beliefs and strive for positive social and environmental impact. This could include companies that value sustainability, diversity, and inclusion, as well as those trying to address important societal challenges.

In addition to investing, your financial goals should be consistent with your principles. If you appreciate independence, you may want to save enough to retire early or pursue a passion project. If you value security, you may want to save for an emergency or pay off debt. Remember that matching your finances and values is an ongoing process. Your financial decisions should evolve in tandem with your changing values and priorities. Assess your financial condition on a regular basis and make necessary modifications to guarantee that your money is supporting your values and ambitions.

Aligning your finances with your principles allows you to make more deliberate decisions about how you earn, save, and spend money. You'll feel more secure and purposeful about your financial decisions, and you'll live a life that matches your beliefs and objectives.

6.2: Pursuing Your Passions and Living a Fulfilling Life

Pursuing your hobbies and leading a fulfilling life involves courage, determination, and a willingness to take risks. It is not always an easy path, but it is highly rewarding and leads to a life with purpose and meaning. Imagine waking up every morning full of enthusiasm and anticipation because you get to spend the day doing something you enjoy. Imagine feeling completely alive, with energy and enthusiasm radiating from every pore. This is what it means to follow your passions and live a fulfilled life.

But how do you go to this location? How can you identify your hobbies and develop them into a career or lifestyle that makes you happy and satisfied? The first step is to listen to your heart and focus on what really interests you. Which activities make you feel the most alive? What are the themes that you incessantly think about? What ideals do you hope to uphold in your life and career?

Once you've identified your passions, the next step is to begin exploring ways to pursue them. This could include taking seminars or workshops, looking for mentors or role models, or simply jumping in and starting to experiment and learn by doing. It's vital to be patient and kind to yourself while you go through this process, which is often full of twists and turns and unanticipated hurdles.

As you start pursuing your passions, you will most certainly face challenges and setbacks. You may experience self-doubt, criticism from others, or financial worry. But it is precisely in these moments that you must summon your strength and will to continue going forward. Remember why you started this trip in the first place, and allow that passion and enthusiasm carry you through the difficult times.

Living a fulfilling life entails not only pursuing your passions, but also developing a feeling of purpose and meaning. This includes recognizing your values and priorities and making decisions that are consistent with them. It entails cultivating strong interpersonal relationships and making important contributions to your community. It entails caring for your physical, emotional, and spiritual well-being, as well as finding methods to unwind and recharge in a fast-paced and often chaotic society.

You'll know when you're living a fulfilled life. You'll get a sense of fulfillment and satisfaction from knowing you're on the correct path. You'll be proud of who you're becoming and the influence you're making on the world around you. You will be grateful for the chances you have and the individuals who have helped and encouraged you along the road.

So, if you're feeling trapped or unfulfilled, realize that it's never too late to change. Take a step back, consider your passions and principles, and begin investigating ways to pursue them. It may not be easy, but it will be worthwhile. Because when you live a life that is authentic to who you are, you will be astounded by the joy, purpose, and fulfillment that result.

6.3: Giving Back and Making a Positive Impact

Giving back and having a positive impact is an effective way to live a life of purpose and meaning. It allows you to use your time, talent, and resources to alter the world and leave a lasting legacy. Giving back helps both others and yourself. You feel accomplished and delighted when you know you're making a difference.

Imagine being able to improve someone's life. Consider being able to help a youngster acquire an education or support a family with clean water and food. Imagine being able to help a cause you are passionate about while knowing that your efforts are making a real difference. Giving back and having a good influence entails more than just providing money or time; it also entails leveraging your unique skills and talents to help others. It's about taking an active role in your community and working to make the world a better place.

When you give back, you benefit not just others, but also yourself. You're making connections and interactions with others, and you're discovering a sense of purpose and significance. You are also acquiring new skills and obtaining new experiences, which will benefit you in all aspects of your life.

Giving back and having a positive impact is also an excellent method to motivate others to do the same. When you show others that giving back is essential to you, they are more inclined to follow suit. You may have a positive impact on the world by spreading love and giving.

So, select a subject you are passionate about and get engaged. Volunteer your time, donate money, and use your unique skills and talents to make a great difference. You never know what impact you'll have on people's lives. And who knows, you might even discover a new sense of purpose and significance in your life.

PART 7: OVERCOMING OBSTACLES AND STAYING MOTIVATED

7.1: Overcoming Financial Setbacks and Staying Disciplined

Overcoming financial setbacks and maintaining discipline takes a combination of tenacity, determination, and sound money management. Financial setbacks can be unexpected and unforeseen, but with the appropriate mindset and methods, you can recover stronger and more financially solid than before. First and foremost, recognize that financial setbacks are a normal part of life. Everyone is vulnerable to unforeseen bills, job losses, and market downturns. The goal is to remain calm, appraise the situation, and devise a strategy for overcoming the setback.

One of the most important aspects in overcoming financial setbacks is to maintain discipline. This entails sticking to your financial objectives and avoiding rash decisions that can jeopardize your success. It's easy to become caught up in the emotions of a financial loss, but it's critical to stay focused and committed to your long-term objectives. To maintain discipline, you must have a thorough awareness of your financial status. This includes keeping track of your income, expenses, and debt, as well as analyzing your financial situation on a regular basis. Staying informed allows you to find areas where you may cut costs, optimize your spending, and make adjustments to get back on track.

Another important part of managing financial disasters is having an emergency fund in place. This money should be utilized for unforeseen needs like auto repairs, medical bills, or job loss. Having an emergency savings fund can help you avoid debt and provide peace of mind during unpredictable times. In addition to having an emergency fund, it is critical to prioritize your spending and concentrate on necessary needs. This entails reducing non-essential costs such as dining out, entertainment, and hobbies and channeling those funds toward your financial objectives.

Maintaining discipline also entails avoiding lifestyle inflation. As your income rises, you may find yourself tempted to spend more on luxuries and enhancements. However, this can soon spiral into a cycle of overspending and debt. Instead, use excess income to achieve your financial goals, such as debt repayment, emergency fund building, or future investment. Overcoming financial losses necessitates a commitment to learn from your mistakes and adjust to changing circumstances. This includes being open to new ideas, receiving guidance from financial professionals, and being willing to change your strategy as necessary.

Finally, maintaining discipline necessitates a long-term outlook. Financial setbacks are usually temporary, and with the correct mindset and methods, you can overcome them and emerge stronger and more financially solid than before. By staying focused on your long-term goals and avoiding rash mistakes, you may create a brighter financial future and attain the financial freedom you deserve.

7.2: Staying Motivated and Focused on Your Goals

Maintaining motivation and focus on your goals is critical to attaining success in any area of your life. Starting strong is easy, but keeping momentum and drive can be difficult. However, with the correct mindset and tactics, you may remain motivated and focused on your goals even when faced with challenges and failures.

One essential component of staying motivated is having a clear and compelling vision of what you want to accomplish. This entails establishing clear, quantifiable, and attainable goals that are consistent with your values and passions. When you have a clear vision, you will be more motivated to take action and achieve your goals. Another crucial component is to divide your goals into smaller, more doable activities. This will allow you to gain momentum and a sense of success as you complete each activity. It's also important to prioritize your duties, focusing on the most important ones first, and to build a timetable that will keep you on track.

Staying motivated also necessitates a positive attitude and a growth mindset. This entails accepting challenges and seeing failure as an opportunity for growth and learning. When you have a positive outlook, you will be more resilient in the face of challenges and more likely to recover from setbacks. Furthermore, surrounding oneself with individuals who believe in you and your goals can be a strong motivation. A network of like-minded people who share your interests and values can offer support, accountability, and motivation.

Staying focused is also critical to achieving your goals. This means minimizing distractions, avoiding procrastination, and staying present in the moment. You can do this by creating a conducive work environment, using tools like the Pomodoro Technique to stay focused, and taking regular breaks to recharge and refocus.

Finally, celebrating your progress and achievements along the way is essential to staying motivated and focused. Recognizing your successes, no matter how small, will help you stay positive and encouraged, and will provide a sense of accomplishment and fulfillment.

Implementing these tactics will allow you to remain motivated and focused on your goals even when faced with obstacles and failures. Remember, success is a journey, not a destination, and keeping motivated and focused is essential for realizing your maximum potential.

7.3: Building a Supportive Community and Network

Creating a supportive community and network is similar to establishing a strong bridge that connects you to a world of opportunities. It's a foundation that offers stability, encouragement, and tools to help you navigate life's problems and enjoy its successes. A solid community and network might mean the difference between feeling isolated and empowered, or suffering and thriving.

Consider having a network of individuals that actually care about your well-being, understand your interests and values, and are committed to your achievement. They offer advice, share their knowledge, and create a safe environment in which to experiment and take chances. They keep you accountable, motivated, and focused on your objectives. They serve as a sounding board for your ideas, a source of comfort in times of need, and a stimulus for growth and learning.

That is what a helpful community and network can provide. It's a web of ties that goes beyond casual acquaintances, a network of people dedicated to mutual support and upliftment. It's a place where you may express yourself without fear of being judged or rejected. Where you may share your experience, your challenges, and your goals, knowing that you will be welcomed with empathy, understanding, and support.

However, creating such a community and network requires effort and intention. It calls for vulnerability, empathy, and a desire to listen and learn. It entails venturing outside of your comfort zone, attending events, joining groups, and participating in discussions that challenge and enrich your viewpoints. It entails being open to feedback, constructive criticism, and fresh ideas while also being willing to provide the same in return.

However, creating such a community and network requires effort and intention. It calls for vulnerability, empathy, and a desire to listen and learn. It entails venturing outside of your comfort zone, attending events, joining groups, and participating in discussions that challenge and enrich your viewpoints. It entails being open to feedback, constructive criticism, and fresh ideas while also being willing to provide the same in return.

A supportive group and network can also give you a sense of belonging, of being a part of something bigger than yourself. It serves as a reminder that you are not alone in your troubles or successes, and that others understand and support you. It provides inspiration, encouragement, and accountability, allowing you to stay focused on your objectives and aspirations.

In today's fast-paced, often alienating environment, establishing a supporting group and network is more crucial than ever. It's a way to balance out the bad effects of social media, the 24-hour news cycle, and the ever-changing demands of work and life. It's a method to create meaningful relationships, discover purpose and meaning, and live a more full, connected existence.

So take the first step now. Attend a local event, join a club based on your interests, or contact someone you like or wish to learn from. Be open, vulnerable, and ready to listen and learn.

As you grow your community and network, you'll uncover a world of opportunities and individuals that care about your success. And you'll understand that, together, you can accomplish everything you set your mind to.

SAVE, MAKE MORE MONEY

PART 8: PUTTING IT ALL TOGETHER

8.1: Creating a Long-Term Financial Plan

Creating a long-term financial plan is similar to beginning on a journey to achieve financial freedom. It's a road plan that will help you negotiate the ups and downs of life, as well as the economic and market fluctuations. With a clear plan in place, you'll be able to make informed decisions that correspond with your aims and beliefs while avoiding costly mistakes that can stymie your development.

Imagine having clarity and certainty about your financial future. You know exactly where you want to go and have a detailed plan for getting there. You can save for your children's education, pay off your mortgage, and establish a retirement fund. You can pursue your hobbies and live the life you've always desired, free from the constraints of financial hardship.

This is what a long-term financial plan can provide. It is a thorough method that considers your income, expenses, assets, and liabilities before recommending a specific strategy to help you achieve your financial objectives. It's a dynamic plan that adapts to changes in your life and the market, allowing you to stay on track and attain your goal.

However, developing a long-term financial strategy involves more than a few quick calculations and a broad sketch. It takes a thorough understanding of your financial status, objectives, and market. It necessitates a dedication to discipline and patience, as well as the ability to adapt and modify when circumstances change. The first step toward developing a long-term financial strategy is to evaluate your current financial condition. This entails compiling all of your financial paperwork, such as income statements, balance sheets, and investment accounts. It entails critically examining your spending patterns, debt, and credit score. It also entails identifying areas for improvement and optimization in your financial performance.

Next, you'll need to determine your financial objectives and priorities. What are you aiming to accomplish? Is it saving for a down payment on a house, repaying student loans, or establishing a retirement account? What are your values and priorities? Do you want to prioritize saving for your kids' education or paying off your mortgage? Once you have a clear grasp of your financial condition and goals, you can start creating a complete plan. This will entail defining a budget, investing in a diverse portfolio, and devising a risk-management strategy to maximize returns. It will also include constantly assessing and updating your plan to ensure that you stay on track and attain your goals.

A long-term financial strategy is not something you do once and then forget about. It's a dynamic and continuing process that necessitates regular monitoring and adjustment. It is a journey, not a destination, and takes discipline and patience. However, the results are definitely worth the effort. With a long-term financial plan in place, you may attain financial independence and live the life you've always desired. You'll be able to pursue your passions, travel, and enjoy the results of your efforts. Furthermore, you will be able to leave a lasting legacy for your loved ones. So, why wait? Begin developing your long-term financial plan today and take the first step toward reaching financial independence and living the life you've always desired.

8.2: Reviewing and Adjusting Your Progress

Reviewing and correcting your progress is similar to driving a meandering road, with each twist and turn revealing a new panorama of opportunities. It's a voyage of self-discovery in which you confront your strengths and flaws and make intentional decisions to guide yourself toward your objectives. As you reflect on your development, you will see both moments of triumph and moments of struggle. You'll find that certain paths you've traveled have resulted in dead ends, while others have opened up new possibilities. You will notice that some habits you have developed have moved you forward, while others have held you back.

Reviewing and adjusting your progress involves more than just acknowledging mistakes; it's also about recognizing patterns and habits that have held you back and making a conscious decision to change. It's about embracing the uncertainty of the journey and trusting that every detour and setback is an opportunity to grow and learn. As you adjust your course, the landscape of your life shifts, opening up new possibilities.

But the trip does not stop there. Reviewing and adjusting your progress is a constant process that involves growth and transformation. It's a reminder that life is a journey, not a destination, and that every moment is an opportunity to learn, adapt, and evolve. So, take a deep breath and begin this path of self-discovery. Examine your progress and change your route. Accept the uncertainty and believe that each step you take will bring you closer to your goals. Remember, the only constant is change, and the only limit is the one you set for yourself.

8.3: Achieving Financial Freedom and Living a Life of Purpose

Many people dream of achieving financial freedom and living a purposeful life, but only a few achieve it. It is a journey that requires devotion, resilience, and a clear grasp of what is actually important in life. Those who persevere, however, will reap immense rewards. Imagine waking up every morning full of excitement and purpose, knowing you have the freedom to pursue your passions and make a positive difference in the world. Imagine having enough money to support your loved ones, travel, and try new things without being burdened by debt or financial concern.

This is what financial independence and a life of purpose look like. It's a life free of the confines of a 9-to-5 work, unrestricted by the quantity of money in your bank account, and undefined by the items you own. It's a life where you can be yourself, follow your aspirations, and make a difference in the world. However, living a life of freedom and purpose takes more than just a desire for it. It necessitates a willingness to take risks, question the status quo, and go past your comfort zone. It demands a dedication to learning, growing, and self-improvement, as well as a readiness to adapt and evolve in the face of uncertainty

It also requires a clear grasp of what is actually important in life. It's easy to get caught up in the pursuit of money and material stuff, but true fulfillment comes from living a life with purpose and meaning. It comes from following your passions, cultivating great relationships, and making a positive difference in the world. So, how do you achieve financial freedom while also living a purposeful life? It begins with a mental shift. It all starts with realizing that you have the ability to build the life you want and that you are not bound by your existing situation. It all starts with identifying clear goals and priorities, and then taking purposeful action to achieve them.

It also requires a dedication to financial literacy and responsibility. It entails learning how to manage your money, invest for the future, and create a safety net to protect yourself from unexpected setbacks. It entails being deliberate with your spending and making mindful decisions that are consistent with your values and aspirations. However, financial freedom and a life of meaning are more than just money. They are about living a life that is authentic to who you are and consistent with your values and passions. They are about following your dreams and making a significant difference in the world. They are about leading a life full of purpose, joy, and fulfillment.

So, what's keeping you from reaching financial independence and a life of purpose? Is it fear, doubt, or uncertainty? Is there a shortage of information or resources? Whatever it is, understand that you have the ability to conquer it. Recognize that you have the potential to design the life you desire and live a life that is authentic to who you are. Take the first step now. Begin by establishing clear goals and priorities, and then taking purposeful action to achieve them. Begin by learning about personal finance and investment, and then make conscious decisions that reflect your values and aspirations. Begin by pursuing your passions and making a meaningful difference in the world.

Remember that financial freedom and a life of meaning are more than just dreams; they are attainable realities. So get out there and make it happen. Make decisions, take risks, and pursue your dreams with passion and purpose. You've got this!

Conclusion

Achieving financial independence and living a life of meaning involves determination, resilience, and a clear awareness of what is actually important. It's a challenging journey that also offers opportunity for growth, learning, and fulfillment. Individuals can break free from the confines of debt and financial stress by establishing clear goals and priorities, allowing them to live a life that is authentic to themselves. A life in which people may pursue their passions, form great relationships, and have a good impact on the world.

Developing a development mindset is critical on this path because it enables people to accept difficulties, learn from failures, and adapt to changing circumstances. Surrounding oneself with a supportive group and network is also important since it offers encouragement, guidance, and accountability. Developing a long-term financial strategy and frequently monitoring progress is critical to reaching financial independence. It enables people to make informed decisions, avoid costly mistakes, and remain focused on their objectives. Individuals can make their ambitions come true by taking strategic risks and following their passions.

Financial freedom and a life of meaning are more than just pipe fantasies; they are attainable. Individuals can build the life they want by taking conscious action, resulting in a life full of purpose, joy, and fulfillment. So, let's take the first step today and begin creating a life that is actually meaningful.

SAVE,MAKE MORE MONEY

www.ingramcontent.com/pod-product-compliance
Lightning Source LLC
Chambersburg PA
CBHW050118230526
45470CB00004B/1889